MONSTER!

For Celia.
C.M.

For Digby.
A.McA.

SIMON AND SCHUSTER

First published in Great Britain in 2005 by Simon & Schuster UK Ltd
Africa House, 64-78 Kingsway, London WC2B 6AH

Text copyright © 2005 Angela McAllister
Illustrations copyright © 2005 Charlotte Middleton

Book designed by Genevieve Webster
The text for this book is set in EggCream and Clarendon
The illustrations are rendered in collage

A CIP catalogue record for this book is available from
the British Library upon request

ISBN 0-689-86078-1
Printed in China
1 3 5 7 9 10 8 6 4 2

MONSTER!

Angela McAllister and Charlotte Middleton

SIMON AND SCHUSTER

London · New York · Sydney

Jackson was always asking his mum and dad to get him a pet. "I want a pet. I have to have a pet. I neeeed a pet. Everyone has a pet," said Jackson.

"Pleeeease?"

"Get a worm out of the garden," said Dad.

"Why not bring home the class rabbit
for the weekend?" suggested Mum.

"**No!**" said Jackson.

"I don't want a worm or a weekend rabbit. I want a pet that's **big** and all mine.

It's got to be **wild** and **exciting!**"

Dad bought Jackson a hamster.

"He's all yours so take care of him."

"You must promise to give him plenty of food," said Mum, "and fresh water and exercise every day. And his cage must be cleaned out on Saturdays."

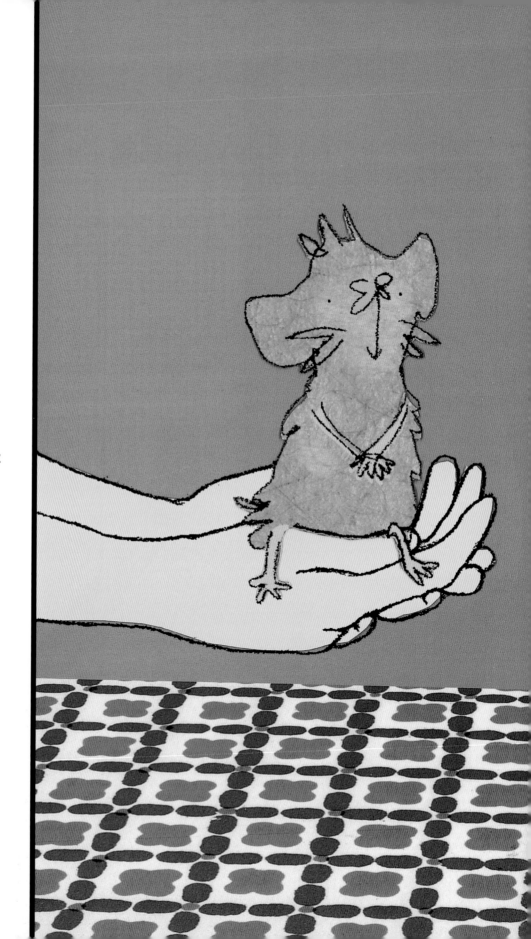

"I promise," said Jackson, with a grudging look.

Jackson named his pet 'Monster'. Jackson tried to train Monster to fetch a stick but Monster wouldn't budge.

Jackson tried to teach him to climb a tree but Monster just sat there.

Jackson even showed Monster how to roar,

Roar!

but Monster buried himself in his bed and
wouldn't come out, not even for a bone.

On Saturday, Jackson forgot to clean out Monster's cage.

Then he forgot to change his water.

By the end of the week Jackson had enough pocket money to buy an old skateboard at the school fete and forgot to feed Monster altogether.

Down in the
shed Monster
got bored
and lonely.

He started to
feel hungry.

Up in his room
Jackson got ready
for bed.

Monster nibbled the latch of his cage, pushed open the door and jumped into the bag of hamster food.

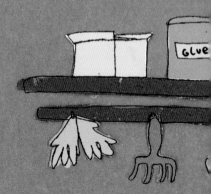

When he'd finished
the hamster food
he explored
the garden . . .

...Jackson, busy doing skateboard stunts in the back garden, didn't even notice Monster growing **big** and **wild** and **exciting...**

...until they both
noticed each other.

"**WOW!** That's the sort of pet I want!"

"Oh dear," sighed Mum. "Well, promise you'll look after him. He needs plenty of food and fresh water and exercise every day, and he must be cleaned on Saturdays."

"I promise!" said Monster.

Monster took Jackson to his den. Monster tried
to teach Jackson to store food in his cheeks.
Monster tried to teach him to run round in a wheel.

Monster even showed Jackson how to build a nest,
but Jackson climbed into a big flowerpot and
wouldn't come out, not even for a bone.

Monster forgot to clean Jackson.
Monster forgot to change Jackson's
water or give him fresh bedding.
Before long, Monster found the
skateboard and forgot about
Jackson altogether.

Down in the
den Jackson got
bored and lonely.

He started to
feel hungry.
Then he heard
a voice.

"Breakfast!" called Mum.
Jackson pushed open the door
of Monster's den and . . .

Jackson rushed downstairs but didn't stop for breakfast.

He ran out to the shed.

Jackson picked up Monster and gave him a handful of food. "From now on I'm going to call you Fluffy," he said. Fluffy looked up at Jackson and gave a small, contented squeak.